ARMS AND ARMOUR

It is only to be expected that, across 2,000 years of history from the Romans to modern-day, arms and armour in Britain should change. However, it may be surprising that some older types of weaponry are still used in a new form, and other items of military equipment have made a full circle – falling out of style, only to come back again. This is true of armour and helmets, although those today are made of synthetic materials.

Firearms had a significant impact on the battlefield and, such was their power, their dominance over all else was assured. There was a brief period when firearms and other weapons such as bows were used in combination, but as guns became more powerful other weapons fell into disuse. But through all this time, bladed weapons such as swords and bayonets continued.

The modern British soldier has many varied duties ranging from ceremonial guard duty to providing humanitarian aid. Nevertheless, the Army is primarily a fighting force and its men and women must always be well equipped and ready for combat.

Charge of the Heavy Brigade at the Battle of Balaclava on 25 October 1854. A force of only 600 British cavalry troops from the regiments of the Scots Greys and Enniskillen Dragoons attacked a superior force of 2,000 Russian cavalry during the Crimean War. The action was fought at such close quarters that only swords could be used with any effect.

THE ROMANS

▼▼▼▼▼▼▼

A centurion's helmet, embossed with the eagle motif. Although helmets evolved during the Roman period, they all aimed to combine protection with comfort. ◀

▲▲▲▲▲▲▲▲▲

A re-creation of Roman legionnaires showing mail armour, hamata, *and the more familiar plate armour,* lorica segmentata. *They are holding* pilum *javelins for throwing and the curved* scutum *shield.* ▲

In AD 43 the Roman army finally settled in Britain; they brought with them a whole new method of conducting warfare which was totally unknown to the local tribes. The Roman Army was essentially an infantry force, and as such, they were equipped with weapons and armour to suit their role on the battlefield.

2

The Roman legionnaire wore armour called *lorica segmentata* which was made from strips of metal strapped together to protect the torso. Another form of armour was the *lorica hamata*, made of metal rings interconnected to produce a chain-mail shirt. Later on, a third type of armour, *lorica squamata*, made from scale-like strips of armour, was introduced. Various styles of helmets were worn during the Roman Empire, usually made from bronze, and decorated with garnitures to indicate rank and unit.

The soldiers carried the *gladius* short-bladed stabbing sword on the right and a dagger on the left. The cavalry used a longer-bladed sword, the *spatha*. A curved shield, *scutum*, was held and this could be overlapped with others for protection of the unit in a manoeuvre called the *testudo*. Early Romans carried a spear called the *hasta*, but it was replaced by the *pilum* which was designed specifically for throwing. It had a wooden shaft to which was fitted a long metal rod tipped with a barbed head; it had great penetrating power.

ROMAN SHIELDS

The curved design of the *scutum* gave maximum protection to the Roman soldier and allowed flexibility in battle. By using their shields as mobile walls the Roman infantry formed a *testudo* and so could move in well-protected formations to meet almost any enemy and defeat them. The oval-shaped, flat shield carried by the auxiliary troops for protection was not as versatile as the *scutum*.

▼▼▼▼▼▼▼▼▼▼▼▼

The tombstone of Rufus Sita, a Roman cavalryman from the 1st century AD. The stone image shows the rider using his spear in an overhand stabbing action. He wears a helmet and carries a spatha, a long-bladed sword, and shield. Note that there were no stirrups at this time. ▼

ROMAN SWORDS

The *gladius* entered service in about 200 BC and the design is known to have been influenced by a Spanish weapon. It was used in a stabbing motion because the Romans understood a penetrating wound was more deadly than a cutting stroke. The longer *spatha* was influenced by the Celtic-style sword and had to be used in a slashing action by the cavalry because of their increased height. The length of the blade could be 80 centimetres (31 inches) and it entirely replaced the *gladius* during the later period of the Empire. At the same time the sword began to be carried on the left side.

THE
DARK AGES

When the Roman legions departed from the shores of Britain between AD 407 and 450, they left behind stocks of armour and weapons, which were seized by many of the 'Romanised' local tribes to save them making new equipment. Their swords remained straight-bladed, but the shields became more simple and round.

By 450 Britain was being raided by European tribes such as the Angles, Saxons and Jutes, each of whom brought with them influences in armour and weapons. This period is known as the Dark Ages and it is during this time that the semi-legendary figure of King Arthur is believed to have reigned.

In 789 the first Viking raiding parties landed in Britain, having crossed the North Sea in long ships rowed from Denmark. They wielded new weapons – short-handled axes to chop or crush their opponent and spears with short-socketed heads fitted to wooden shafts. But it was the long, heavy-bladed Frankish sword with straight sides which was to have the greatest influence on British

◀ ◀ ◀ ◀ ◀
These long, straight-bladed Viking swords were recovered from an archaeological dig. The pattern is very simple to manufacture and influenced the shape of swords for hundreds of years. ◀

▼ ▼ ▼ ▼ ▼ ▼ ▼ ▼
Every year the Jorvik Viking Festival in York re-enacts the capture of the city by Viking warriors in 866. These warriors are carrying round shields typical of the period, axes and straight-bladed swords. ▼

weaponry. The Vikings also had archers with short bows and, for more mobility on land, they used horses. The Vikings wore no armour in battle apart from some mail-armour shirts, and relied instead on helmets and their round shields for protection. Contrary to popular belief the Viking helmets did not feature horns or other affectations.

From 851 the Vikings established the first settlements in Britain, but their warlike raiding continued. Viking power in Britain was finally broken when King Edward defeated them in 914 and killed Guthrum II in battle.

The Anglo-Saxon tribes now became the dominant power in the country and adopted weapons used by the Vikings, such as the axe. Helmets remained largely open-fronted, but other designs incorporated masks to protect the wearer's face. Mail armour was further developed into a garment which reached to the knees and in some cases included a head covering. This item was known as a *byrnie* and was later called a *hauberk*.

▲▲▲▲▲▲▲▲▲▲▲

A replica of the Sutton Hoo helmet, so-called because of the site in Norfolk where it was discovered in 1939. Dating from the 7th century, it was probably the ceremonial helmet of a clan chieftain. ▲

▼▼▼▼▼▼▼▼▼▼▼▼

This scene shows a Saxon battle. The swords have long, straight blades; the shields are round with reinforced central boss and some soldiers are wearing 'Phrygian'-style caps popular at the time. ▼

VIKING AXES

The axe used by the Vikings was the *skeggox* or 'bearded axe'. It came into use in about the 7th century and evolved into the broad-headed type, with a longer handle. It soon spread across Europe and into Britain, where it was recognised as a useful close-quarter weapon.

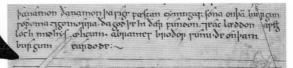

THE
NORMANS

Axes and maces were the main crushing weapons used by the invading Normans. The cavalry particularly favoured the long-handled mace, shown on the left. ▲

Despite the fact that Viking communities had settled in Britain, the main body in Norway and Denmark remained a military threat. This uneasy peace lasted until 1066 when King Harold led a force northwards to meet and decisively defeat a huge Viking invasion at the Battle of Stamford Bridge on 25 September that year. At the Battle of Hastings on 14 October 1066 Harold then led his army against a French invasion, led by William of Normandy.

The two armies wore chain-mail armour for body protection, with some types, known as *hauberks*, reaching to the knees. Both sides wore conical helmets, under which was worn a padded head-piece and a mail hood called a *coif*. The French carried kite-shaped shields while the English had either round or oval shields strapped to their left arms.

▼▼▼▼▼▼▼▼▼
This carving from the Temple Pyx (thought to have belonged to the Knights Templar) shows typical equipment of the period, including a lance, kite-shaped shield and a straight-bladed sword. ▼

AD PRELIVM: CON TRA

The troops which formed this unit were considered the personal bodyguard of the king. The first housecarls were raised in 1016 and were paid by means of *heregeld*, or army tax, and received grants of land. At Hastings, King Harold's housecarls formed around his position on Senlac Hill and wielded their long-handled axes in a two-handed 'figure-of-eight' motion which cut through everything. They continued to fight even after Harold was killed, and stood almost to the last man.

▼▼▼▼▼▼▼▼▼
Scene from the Battle of Hastings, represented on the Bayeux Tapestry in France. The Norman cavalry wear mail armour and conical helmets with nasal guard, and hold their lances couched. They now have stirrups fitted to the saddle to give them better balance and control of the horse. ▼

The French fought on foot and horseback, but the English preferred fighting on foot. The mounted French carried their lances in a couched position, tucked under the arm to take the impact when striking a target, and their shields were suspended by a strap which passed over the shoulder.

Both armies used heavy-bladed straight swords and some troops carried axes. The bow was also used by both sides and it was a French archer who inflicted the mortal wound to Harold. Clubs, called maces, were beginning to emerge as weapons. Used by the French, these were either long or short-handled and were purely crushing weapons.

Harold's army was defeated and the influence of French weapons, tactics and armour spread across the country as William's army advanced. Mounted troops in future would benefit from having improved saddles and stirrups for better balance and the long lances used by other European armies. Chain-mail armour would remain the most widely used form of body protection for over 200 years, until plate armour started to come into fashion.

▲▲▲▲▲▲▲▲▲
This scene from a 12th-century illuminated manuscript in Durham Cathedral shows Norman knights using straight-bladed swords in battle. ▲

THE CRUSADES

▲▲▲▲▲▲▲▲▲

This 13th-century manuscript shows the crossbow being used during the siege of a castle. The fact that large numbers of men could be trained in its use very quickly made up for its slowness in action. ▲

In 1095 Pope Urban II called on Christian warriors to retake the Holy Land from the Muslims who had occupied it since 638. The crusades, therefore, were Christian military expeditions to the Middle East undertaken by Western European kings and knights. The first crusade in 1096 was followed by a further seven over the next 300 years.

In around 1120 England created special groups for the crusades: the Orders of the Knights Templar and St John. Both wore loose-fitting surcoats over their chain-mail armour. The Order of St John had the identifying emblem of a white cross on a red surcoat while the Knights Templar wore a red Cross of Jerusalem on their white surcoats. These knights used the sword as a symbol of their position, but men-at-arms – the foot soldiers – used crossbows, polearms and swords. Because of the hot climate, the knights wore chain-mail armour and conical helmets of the Norman-style.

THE CROSSBOW

The crossbow, although widely used and accurate, was never popular due to its slow rate of shooting arrows. In 1139 Pope Innocent II tried to ban the use of the weapon against Christians, but the ban was never fully implemented. In 1100, William Rufus, king of England, had been murdered by a crossbow and in 1199 another English king, Richard the Lionheart, was killed at Chalus by a crossbow as he was returning from a crusade.

▶▶▶▶▶▶▶▶

A 12th-century drawing of a crusader. He is wearing armour of mail hauberk and holding a lance, a type of polearm. ▶

A Knight Templar charging into battle in 1163. He holds his lance in the couched position and wears a surcoat over his mail armour. The kite-shaped shield is still evident as is the conical helmet with nasal guard. ▼

King William Rufus was killed by a crossbow arrow in 1100 whilst hunting in the New Forest in modern-day Hampshire. In the Magna Carta of 1215, King John outlawed foreign crossbowmen in England, but the weapon continued to be used to defend castles. ▲

East meets West: unprotected Muslim cavalry fight crusaders in mail armour and iron helmets. The crusaders are using straight-bladed swords and their shields are a small 'cut-down' kite shape, which was easier to control on horseback. ▲

The Battle of Agincourt. The English longbow dominated the battlefield by virtue of its range, hitting power and the volume of arrows shot by the archers. ▲

THE LONGBOW

The longbow was introduced from Wales and made from the wood of yew trees. It had a range of 400 metres (440 yards) and some archers could fire over ten arrows per minute. The bow was 1.8 metres (6 feet) long and required about 90 kilograms (200lbs) of pull to shoot the arrows. By law every male in the land had to be well versed in the use of this powerful weapon.

Plate armour became more developed from the 14th century onwards and was extended to protect all parts of the body, including the hands. Armour was formed of different pieces secured together by leather straps with special names to identify each piece, such as the vambrace to protect the lower arm and pauldrons which protected the shoulders.

Helmets developed into various types, with names such as sallets and bascinets; they could be open-faced or fitted with hinged visors. Armour protection for horses was also developed and this too had its own set of terms, such as the chanfron which protected the horse's head. Later, Henry VIII would bring artisans from Europe to establish workshops at Greenwich where they produced fine suits of armour.

The sword still remained the symbol of the knight's status and of power. The mace and axe were retained and a new type of weapon – the war hammer, with a pick-like point for piercing armour – was introduced. Polearms, such as glaves, and halberds, were used to equip the men-at-arms who carried swords and wore helmets, but had little or no armour.

More use was made of archers and the crossbow was supplemented by the powerful longbow which had a telling effect during the Hundred Years' War at battles such as Poitiers in 1356 and Agincourt in 1415.

Gunpowder weapons were first used by the English army in 1346, when some crude and inaccurate cannons were fired at the Battle of Crecy. These early handguns were fired by means of applying a lighted match to a hole in the barrel and were thus termed 'matchlocks'.

◀◀◀◀◀◀◀◀◀◀◀◀

War hammers were used by mounted knights to pierce plate armour. Introduced from France and Italy, this crushing weapon was capable of inflicting terrible puncture wounds to all parts of the body. ◀

▲▲▲▲▲▲▲▲▲▲

The Battle of Crecy. Early gunpowder weapons, such as cannons, were beginning to be used. The man in the lower right of the picture is using a curved sword called a falchion, which was designed to break open plate armour. ▲

ARROWHEADS

Each archer carried some 24 arrows of the 'yard cloth' length (0.915 metres) which could be fitted with various types of head. The long, thin bodkin, shown in the centre, was designed to penetrate armour, while a crescent-shaped head was used to shred the sails of ships. The broadhead (right) was for other targets. Other special heads were designed for hunting and as fire-arrows.

JOUSTING
TOURNAMENTS

A knight constantly had to practise for battle and so the joust was developed in which a man pitted his skills against training devices or other knights. These training exercises were the closest thing to real combat a knight was to experience outside battle.

In 1194 Richard I, himself an enthusiastic jousting combatant, legalised tournaments in England. Judges and heralds were appointed to keep order at meetings and act as adjudicators between combatants. Roger de Hoveden wrote of jousting in the 12th century, 'A youth must have seen his blood flow and felt his teeth crack under the blow of his adversary, and must have been thrown to the ground twenty times, before he is truly capable of facing real war with hope of victory.'

▲▲▲▲▲▲▲▲▲▲▲▲▲▲▲▲
John Chalons, an English knight, and Loys de Beul of France test each other's skill at arms in a joust under the watchful eyes of the ladies of the court. ▲

▶▶▶▶▶▶▶▶▶▶▶▶▶▶▶
Today, re-enactments of jousts are a regular feature at Warwick Castle during the summer months. This rider is charging at a target to test his skills with the lance. ▶

This extravaganza of a royal joust marked a meeting between King Henry VIII and Emperor Maximillian I in 1513. Such mêlées involved hundreds of combatants. Henry VIII was particularly fond of jousting and in 1511 spent over £4,000 on a tournament in Westminster, equivalent to £1.75 million today. ▲

The tournament continued to develop until 1420 when the formal joust was introduced, whereby two knights rode against each other using lances across a wooden barrier known as a 'tilt'. The mêlée was an extension of the joust: a large group of knights entered the arena to give mock battle. Tournaments were supposed to take place only with royal consent but some meetings went ahead without approval and large sums of money might be wagered on the outcome. Special armour, helmet crests and weapons were developed for the tournament. One innovation was the helm, which completely encased the head.

In 1520 the court of Henry VIII travelled to France to meet Francis I in the most famous joust in history, at a meeting called the Field of Cloth of Gold. Only four years later, in March 1524, Henry was almost killed during a jousting tournament. By the end of the 16th century the tournament had become mainly a status symbol for monarchs, and the rising costs meant it could no longer be justified.

THE QUINTAIN

One special training device for the joust was the quintain – a pivoted arm mounted on an upright post. On one end of the arm was a target shield and on the other was a heavy weight. The rider charged the target with his lance and had to follow through very quickly to avoid being hit by the counter-weight as it swung round.

Children became squires and trained to be knights. Here young squires amuse themselves at the quintain and at the same time learn the skills required for jousting. ▲

THE
TUDOR DYNASTY

The whole of the 16th century belongs to the Tudor monarchs, and during this time there was much change in arms and armour. Henry VII, the first Tudor, became king in 1485 at the end of the Wars of the Roses. It had been won with longbows and early handguns, wielded by soldiers who wore a variety of armour and helmets.

In 1485 Henry VII raised the Yeoman of the Guard, the first permanent English military force. Today they are known universally as Beefeaters and they can be seen at the Tower of London in a uniform (shown on page 28) almost unchanged in over 500 years. They traditionally carry a halberd, which has a spear point and an axe-type blade, typical of the weapons carried by foot soldiers in the 16th century.

The armoured knight with sword and lance was still a military force, but arque-busiers using matchlock weapons fitted with firing mechanisms rendered them vulnerable to fire at close range. Nevertheless, armour was still being made at centres such as Greenwich, although bulky armour was beginning to be discarded in favour of speed. Use of the axe was in decline and the mace was now more ceremonial, being carried as a symbol of status.

The crossbow went into decline too, and was used mainly as a hunting weapon. The longbow continued, however, and served alongside increasingly

▶ ▶ ▶ ▶ ▶ ▶ ▶ ▶ ▶ ▶ ▶

A gentleman at arms, or musketeer, of Tudor times. He carries his matchlock musket over his shoulder and, in his right hand, a smouldering match for igniting his weapon. He still wears a sword and, on his right hip, is the powder flask to reload his musket. ▶

◀ ◀ ◀ ◀ ◀ ◀ ◀ ◀ ◀ ◀ ◀ ◀ ◀

Henry VIII established an armouries workshop at Greenwich, where this suit of armour was created for him in 1515. The horse armour includes the chanfron, which protected the animal's head and neck, and glancing bosses on the main chest armour. ◀

more powerful gunpowder weapons. This was confirmed when the *Mary Rose*, Henry VIII's great warship, was raised from the seabed in 1982: marine archaeologists discovered longbows, swords and gunpowder weapons stored in readiness for battle.

▲ ▲ ▲ ▲ ▲ ▲ ▲

Although firearms had become the dominant weapon, the sword was still used for personal protection. This example was recovered from the wreck of the Mary Rose when it was raised in 1982. ▲

◀ ◀ ◀ ◀ ◀ ◀ ◀ ◀

John Derricke's drawing of a marching column of English troops c.1581 shows all the weapons used at the time, including pike, sword and musket for the infantry and lances for the cavalry. They wear breastplates and morion-style helmets. ◀

In 1595, during the reign of Queen Elizabeth, the decision was taken to replace the longbow on the battlefield with handguns such as the arquebus. The arquebusier was protected by a helmet, breastplate and backplate, and in addition to his matchlock weapon also carried a sword and dagger for personal protection. Polearms, such as halberds, glaves and poleaxes, were still used against the cavalry.

Tactical formations of foot soldiers armed with 6-metre (20-foot) long pikes were being massed in blocks to break up cavalry charges. This manoeuvre had been in use in Scotland since the 13th century where they were called schiltrons. In fact, the pike block, as it became known, was to be a feature in the 17th century during the English Civil War.

◀ ◀ ◀ ◀ ◀ ◀ ◀ ◀ ◀

Gunmakers sometimes incorporated guns into devices such as shields and maces as a way of demonstrating their skills. Here three barrels have been concealed in the head of a mace and a single barrel in the boss of a shield, both of which belonged to Henry VIII. ◀

THE ENGLISH
CIVIL WAR

The English Civil War began in 1642 and was essentially a constitutional argument between King and Parliament as to who ruled the country. The belligerents in the war were the Royalists who supported King Charles I and the Parliamentarians, known as 'Roundheads'.

The trend for less armour continued on both sides, especially in the infantry units. However, armour was still favoured by the pikemen who also wore a morion-style helmet with a wide brim. The war proved that gunpowder weapons had complete mastery of the battlefield, especially the matchlock musket, fired by men referred to as musketeers.

◀ ◀ ◀ ◀ ◀ ◀ ◀ ◀ ◀ ◀ ◀ ◀ ◀ ◀

Swords continued to have long, straight blades because they were practical in battle. This elaborately decorated sword is from the early 17th century. ◀

▲ ▲ ▲ ▲ ▲ ▲ ▲ ▲

The 'lobster-tail' helmet was worn by officers of the Parliamentarian cavalry. It gave good all-round protection to the head and neck. The reinforcing comb over the skull protected the top of the head. ▲

▲ ▲ ▲ ▲ ▲ ▲ ▲ ▲

This pikeman's helmet was known as a morion. Its basic design was easy to produce and protected the wearer to some extent from blows from above. ▲

◀ ◀ ◀ ◀ ◀ ◀ ◀

A contemporary drawing of Prince Rupert in the service of his uncle Charles I. He wears some armour but no helmet. The pistol he is using was fired at close quarters to ensure hitting the target. ◀

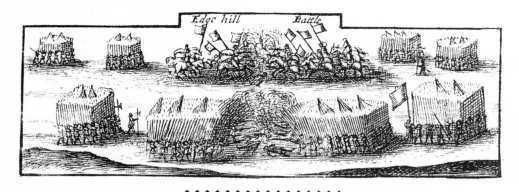

Pike blocks at the Battle of Edgehill, 24 October 1642. The pikes were 16 feet (nearly 5 metres) long, tipped with an iron point. Pike blocks presented cavalry with a bristling row of sharp points. ▲

Huge pike blocks were put into the field by both armies. These powerful formations comprised hundreds of men holding long pikes, grouped into wedges to break up cavalry charges. The pikemen carried swords for self-protection but remained vulnerable to fire from gunpowder weapons, such as muskets and artillery.

Both sides wore almost identical types of uniforms and used similar weaponry. Indeed, on some occasions, coloured armbands or sashes were worn as the only means of identifying each side.

Cavalrymen carried heavy-bladed swords and at least two pistols which could be fired at close range to the pikemen. Riders wore breast and backplates over a thick buff coat which took some of the impact from a sword. Some cavalrymen wore armoured gauntlets to protect their left hands, holding the horses' bridles, from sword cuts.

This re-enactment shows muskets from the period of the English Civil War being fired. Muskets were slow and not very accurate, but firing by massed ranks of musketeers produced many casualties with dreadful wounds. ▲

Parliamentary cavalry wore 'lobster-tail' helmets which had a face guard, or at least an adjustable nasal guard. The Royalist cavalry favoured flamboyant hats, under which some wore iron caps in place of true helmets.

Both sides deployed musketeers who were formed into special units to fire their weapons in blocks. These weapons had a limited range and were not very accurate beyond 50 metres (55 yards). They could fire only once or twice a minute and some were so long they had to be fired from a monopod rest.

ORIGIN OF THE BAYONET

The bayonet is believed to have originated in the French town of Bayonne in 1640. The first types called 'plug bayonets' were long-bladed, dagger-type weapons with a simple handle which allowed it to be inserted into the barrel of the musket after firing. In this way it could be used by musketeers as a substitute for the pike to protect themselves from cavalry charges.

THE
NAPOLEONIC WARS

The Brown Bess musket replaced the matchlock as the main firearm on the battlefield around 1720. This was a flintlock weapon: it used a small piece of flint striking against a steel surface to create a spark to ignite the gunpowder and so fire the musket. The flintlock was a reliable mechanism and was used on naval cannon and on pistols for the cavalry. The Brown Bess was to remain in use with the army until the 1840s and appeared in several models.

Bayonets were now fitted with a long blade of the socket-type which used a collar that fitted over the barrel and so permitted the soldier to carry on loading and firing. The blade was over 45 centimetres (about 18 inches) long and 'cranked' (bent into shape), so that the foot soldier could both fire and protect himself without a pike.

The more accurate Baker rifle was used between 1800 and 1840 by specially raised rifle regiments, which had marksmen who fired like modern day snipers. Sergeants in this period carried staffs called spontoons, which were shortened pikes; they used them to keep the lines of infantry straight and as a symbol of their rank.

▲▲▲▲▲▲▲▲▲
A rifleman of the North York Militia loading a Baker rifle. Designed by Ezekiel Baker, this muzzle-loaded weapon with a flintlock action and rifled barrel was highly accurate up to 200 metres (220 yards). ▲

▼▼▼▼▼▼▼▼▼▼▼
The Brown Bess musket was made in several patterns, including this India Pattern, and used by the British Army for over 120 years. This robust weapon had a flintlock firing mechanism and could be fitted with a socket bayonet, as seen here. ▼

◀◀◀◀◀◀◀◀◀◀◀◀◀◀◀◀◀◀◀◀◀

Lady Butler's painting of the 28th Regiment of Foot, later to become the Gloucestershire Regiment, at the Battle of Waterloo on 18 June 1815. They are forming a square and levelling their bayonet-tipped Brown Bess muskets to fend off an attack by French cavalry. ◀

▶▶▶▶▶▶▶▶▶▶▶▶▶▶

This sword was presented to Lt-Colonel David Stewart of Garth in 1808 and shows how the basket hilt protected the hand during close-quarter cavalry actions. ▶

Armour had all but disappeared from the battlefield, with only the cavalry still wearing breast and backplates. Some regiments, such as The Life Guards, continued to wear helmets, but Hussar regiments wore fur caps called busbies. Infantry regiments did not wear any armour or helmets, but officers wore a device called a gorget at their throat, which, along with their swords, was a symbol of rank rather than a protective device.

Cavalry still carried swords, which by this time were often based on the Scottish full-basket hilt to protect the hand. This was sometimes called the claymore or *claidheamh mor* after a 16th-century style of sword, also of Scottish origin.

The Battle of Waterloo, 18 June 1815, saw every type of army weapon in service used in action. When attacked by cavalry, the infantry formed into impregnable squares out of which they thrust their Brown Bess muskets tipped with bayonets. This tactic was almost identical to the pike block of old and served the same purpose, namely to break up a cavalry charge. Only the most foolish or brave approached this spiked hedge. The battle was a triumph for the use of combined arms, although the Duke of Wellington commented that 'it was a close run thing'.

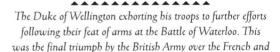

▲▲▲▲▲▲▲▲▲▲▲▲▲▲

The Duke of Wellington exhorting his troops to further efforts following their feat of arms at the Battle of Waterloo. This was the final triumph by the British Army over the French and ended the Napoleonic Wars in Europe. ▲

▲▲▲▲▲▲▲▲▲▲▲▲

Firearms had been used in crimes of robbery since the early 18th century. The flintlock pistol was favoured by highwaymen because it was readily available and easily concealed. ▲

THE
VICTORIAN ARMY

The Victorian period saw the greatest change for the British Army. As technology improved, new and improved firearms were introduced. The first was the Enfield rifled musket in 1853. It was fitted with a rifled barrel for better accuracy, and fired a Minie-type conical bullet of .577 inch calibre. The weapon was muzzle-loaded, but was fired by means of a percussion cap filled with fulminate of mercury to create the spark to fire the weapon.

The first breech-loading weapon for the British Army was the Snider-Enfield rifle, introduced in 1867, and it was followed by the Martini-Henry rifle in 1871 which fired a bullet of .45 inch calibre. In 1888 the bolt-action Lee-Metford rifle entered service. It had a magazine holding ten bullets which could be fired to a range of 2,000 metres (1.2 miles), and established the design which the army would use during both world wars.

To this arsenal was added a new type of weaponry – the machine gun, which provided automatic fire. Bayonets were still used and could be fitted to all rifles of the period. With these weapons, the army fought dozens of actions of varying duration on all continents.

▸▸▸▸▸▸▸▸▸▸▸▸▸▸▸▸
Men of the 72nd Highlanders, today part of the Queen's Own Highlanders, photographed during the Crimean War, 1854–6. They are all holding percussion-fired three-band Enfield muskets, introduced into service in 1852. ▸

▲▲▲▲▲▲▲▲▲
The Scots Fusilier Guards in action during the Crimean War at the Battle of Alma on 20 September 1854. After firing their single bullet, each soldier attacked the enemy with his bayonet, or they used the musket in a clubbing action, as seen on the left. ▲

▲▲▲▲▲▲▲▲▲
Scarlet tunics were replaced by khaki, a more practical colour for a modern army. Scarlet tunics are still worn for ceremonial occasions such as Trooping the Colour. ▲

THE MAXIM MACHINE GUN

Introduced into the British Army in 1889, the Maxim gun could fire 600 rounds per minute, giving an enormous increase in firepower. A jingoistic comment of the day ran, 'Whatever happens we have got, the Maxim gun, and they have not.' It weighed 27 kilograms (60lbs) and worked on the recoil principle, whereby the breech mechanism moved back automatically during firing to extract the spent cartridge case and load another bullet into the chamber ready to fire as it moved forwards. It could reach targets over 2,000 metres (1.2 miles) away.

Uniforms afforded little protection in the extreme cold and were uncomfortable in tropical heat. In 1899 the Second Boer War erupted, sparking changes in the British Army, not only in weapons but also in uniform. To camouflage the troops from enemy observation, the colour of the uniform changed from scarlet to dull khaki, a Persian word in origin, meaning dust or ashes. Lightweight pith helmets were widely worn, but they were not bullet-proof.

Cavalry had already abandoned armour and helmets, except for ceremonial duties, and officers now carried revolvers in addition to their swords. The lance was still carried by some regiments during the Boer War, but by the First World War it had become obsolete.

▲▲▲▲▲▲▲▲▲
Re-creation of khaki-coloured uniforms introduced during the Boer War 1899–1902. The lightweight helmets were manufactured from cork, which gave little protection to the wearer's head. ▲

THE FIRST
WORLD WAR

In 1914 Britain declared war against Germany, when it invaded Belgium. The rifle and bayonet was still the infantryman's basic weapon, but some very powerful weapons were to emerge.

The standard rifle of the time for the British Army was the Short Magazine Lee-Enfield, SMLE, which fired a bullet of .303 inch calibre from a magazine holding ten rounds. The maximum effective range was almost 600 metres (660 yards) and soldiers were trained in shooting practice known as the 'mad minute'. The soldier fired at a target 300 metres (330 yards) away and had to hit it with 15 rounds fired in just one minute. When faced with such firepower the Germans believed the British Army was greatly armed with machine guns. A long-bladed bayonet could be fitted to the rifle and new recruits were rigorously trained in its use.

Infantry regiments had machine guns, such as the Hotchkiss and the Lewis, each

▼▼▼▼▼▼▼▼▼▼▼▼
A sentry at a look-out post at Givenchy, France, in June 1918. His Lee-Enfield rifle, with fitted bayonet, is ready close at hand. ▼

▼▼▼▼▼▼▼▼▼▼▼▼▼
Cavalry was still deployed in the First World War, but artillery and machine guns were so lethal they prevented the mounted units from operating in any useful manner. ▼

of which weighed some 12 kilograms (26lbs) and could fire 550 rounds per minute. In the face of such firepower it was extremely difficult for the enemy to advance towards the British trenches in France. The infantry also used hand grenades called 'Mills bombs' and mortars which were very effective in trench warfare.

Officers carried revolvers, such as the Webley which weighed over a kilogram (2.2lbs) and fired a bullet of .455 inch calibre. Early in the war they carried swords as a symbol of their rank, but this made them a target for enemy snipers: the carrying of swords on the battlefield was then stopped.

In 1915 the British Army re-introduced the steel helmet to protect the men's heads. Although this was the first helmet in more than 250 years, the design was based on the old-fashioned 'kettle helmet' worn by soldiers in the 1400s. Men serving in tanks wore a special mask made from chain-mail to protect their faces, but these were not popular. When poisonous gas was used, all troops had to wear masks as protection and this made conditions very uncomfortable.

Men of the 25th Middlesex Regiment training with the bayonet in England in 1915. ▲

VICKERS MACHINE GUN

The Vickers machine gun, introduced into service in 1912, weighed almost 20 kilograms (44lbs) and was fired from a tripod mount. It fired bullets of .303 inch calibre at the rate of 450 rounds per minute to ranges of almost 1,000 metres (1,093 yards). It was 1.2 metres (4 feet) long, extremely reliable and very popular with the troops, despite its weight. The Vickers remained in service throughout the Second World War and well into the 1960s.

◀ ◀ ◀ ◀ ◀ ◀ ◀ ◀ ◀ ◀ ◀
The Vickers machine gun. The men are wearing gas helmets to protect them from poisonous gas. ◀

THE SECOND
WORLD WAR

▲▲▲▲▲▲▲▲▲

The Home Guard was raised in 1940 and almost 1.75 million men and women served in local units across the country. ▲

In 1939 Britain was again at war with Germany when Poland was invaded. As in the previous war the British infantryman was equipped with a basic bolt-action rifle – the Lee-Enfield No. 4 Mark I, still firing the .303 inch calibre bullet. The bayonet was still issued but became a much shorter, spike-type design. The design of the steel helmet was still the same as in the First World War and special armour plate was available to some infantrymen. Officers no longer carried swords but did carry revolvers.

To counter the threat of invasion by Germany, a volunteer force was raised in 1940. It was known initially as the Local Defence Volunteers, LDV, but later renamed the Home Guard. Men serving in the Home Guard were armed with a variety of weapons of various ages, and wore standard steel helmets. Their weapons included Lewis guns and rifles and also some basic artillery designs such as the Blacker Bombard and the Smith Gun, which was issued in large numbers.

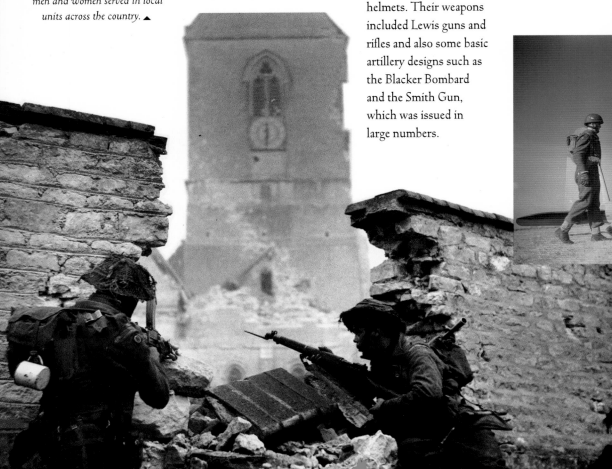

STEN SUB-MACHINE GUN

The Sten sub-machine gun entered service in 1941 and was a relatively simple weapon to use. Over two million in four different marks were manufactured at an estimated cost of only £2.87 per gun. It weighed about 3 kilograms (6.6lbs) and fired a 9mm bullet to a maximum range of 200 metres (220 yards). A popular weapon, the Sten gun was used by soldiers everywhere, including the Parachute Regiment; it was even sent to resistance fighters in Occupied Europe. It continued in service well after the end of the war.

The regular army increased in size during the Second World War and special units were raised, including the Parachute Regiment. These troops were equipped with weaponry to meet most exigencies, including anti-tank weapons such as the Projector Infantry Anti-Tank, PIAT, which could destroy a tank at ranges of 100 metres (110 yards).

Mortars in 2 inch and 3 inch calibres were issued, and machine guns included the Vickers and the newly introduced Bren gun, which could fire up to 500 rounds per minute to ranges of over 800 metres (880 yards). A wide range of grenades was used, from the standard Mills No. 36, which could be thrown by hand or launched from the rifle using a special adaptor, through to the No. 82 'Gammon grenade', used primarily by airborne troops.

◄ ◄ ◄ ◄ ◄ ◄ ◄ ◄

When the Parachute Regiment was raised in 1942, items of equipment and weapons unique to its role were developed, including the glider which these men are boarding and their style of helmet. ◄

▼ ▼ ▼ ▼ ▼ ▼ ▼ ▼ ▼ ▼ ▼ ▼ ▼

It is essential to keep weapons clean in order for them to function properly. Here men of the Green Howards are cleaning their rifles in readiness for D-Day, 6 June 1944. ▼

◄ ◄ ◄ ◄ ◄ ◄ ◄ ◄

Infantry in Europe in 1944 taking cover behind a brick wall. The soldier on the right has a Lee-Enfield rifle while the other soldier has a Bren light machine gun, first introduced in 1937. ◄

POSTWAR YEARS

Since the end of the Second World War in 1945, the British Army has been involved in numerous campaigns around the world. During the Korean War, fought from 1950 to 1953, the British soldier used virtually the same weapons as he had in the Second World War, but since then equipment has changed dramatically. New uniforms and weapons were introduced in the 1960s, and included the semi-automatic rifle known as the L1A1 Self-Loading Rifle (SLR) and a powerful machine gun called a General Purpose Machine Gun (GPMG). Both fired a 7.62mm calibre bullet.

▲▲▲▲▲▲▲▲▲

The General Purpose Machine Gun (GPMG) is used by all branches of Britain's armed forces. Here it is operated by a Royal Marine on HMS Brave *during the 1991 Gulf War.* ▲

FALKLANDS WAR

In 1982 Argentina invaded the British territories of the Falkland Islands in the South Atlantic. All the weaponry at the disposal of the infantry was used in the short but fiercely fought war that followed. This included the SLR, GPMG, hand grenades, anti-tank rockets and mortars. For the first time the infantryman used an anti-aircraft missile called the Blowpipe, which could be fired from the shoulder, and added a new dimension to his firepower. As the troops also faced danger from armoured vehicles, they carried special missiles called Milan which could hit a target at 2,000 metres (1.2 miles). Throughout, soldiers retained their bayonets and wore only steel helmets for personal protection.

▲▲▲▲▲▲▲▲

The 7.62mm L1A1 SLR, as used by the British Army until the late 1980s. It had a 20-round detachable box magazine and could hit targets at over 800 metres (880 yds). ▲

KEVLAR AND BALLISTIC NYLON

Protection for today's soldiers is made from specially developed synthetic textiles, such as Kevlar, which can be formed into body armour (bullet-proof vests) and is lightweight. Helmets are now made from either ballistic nylon or Kevlar and are much stronger and lighter than the old steel helmets.

GULF WAR

A modern infantryman of the 4th Armoured Brigade during the Gulf War in 1991. He is wearing body armour and helmet and holding the SA80 rifle. He is leaning on a LAW94 anti-tank weapon which has an effective range of 500 metres (550 yards). ▼

Eight years later, in 1991, a new generation of soldiers was using a different generation of weaponry to fight in 'Operation Granby'. This was Britain's part of the multi-national Coalition Force poised to attack Iraq after that country had invaded Kuwait. The rifle remained the infantryman's standard weapon, but the new weapon – the SA80 – was much shorter than previously and was designed to a layout known as the 'Bullpup'. This rifle is still in use. It fires a smaller bullet of only 5.56mm calibre as does the fully automatic version of the rifle – the Light Support Weapon.

New anti-aircraft missiles were also deployed along with anti-tank missiles, such as the LAW94 rocket launcher. Infantrymen wore special body armour and new helmets made from nylon. They also had to protect themselves from chemicals by wearing gas masks, as soldiers had done in the First World War.

An infantryman moves towards an Iraqi position during the Gulf War in 1991. He is carrying all his personal equipment and an SA80 rifle which is fitted with a bayonet. ▲

Warwick Castle

Warwick Castle, Warwick CV34 4QU. Tel: 0870 4422000; www.warwick-castle.co.uk Charts 1,000 years of history; a full calendar of special events including displays of archery and jousting.

Royal Armouries Museum, The Waterfront, Leeds LS10 1LT. Tel: 0870 5106666; www.armouries.org.uk Some 3,000 artefacts of weaponry and armour; sword-fighting and jousting during the summer.

Yeoman Warder, Tower of London

Royal Armouries, HM Tower of London, London EC3N 4AB. Tel: 020 7480 6358; www.armouries.org.uk Excellent displays of personal and horse armour as well as weapons. Yeoman Warders (Beefeaters) can be seen all year round.

Windsor Castle, Windsor, Berks SL4 1NJ. Tel: 01753 869898; www.royalresidences.com Historical site; Changing the Guard at 11.00 a.m. on most days.

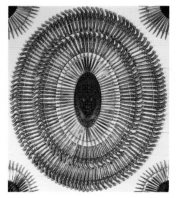

Guard Chamber, Hampton Court Palace

Hampton Court Palace, East Molesey, Surrey KT8 9AU. Tel: 020 8781 9500; www.hrp.org.uk Fine collection of armour and weaponry.

Exhibits in the Imperial War Museum

Imperial War Museum, Lambeth Road, London SE1 6HZ. Tel: 020 7416 5000; www.iwm.org.uk The museum concentrates on both world wars and modern conflict.

Explosion!, Museum of Naval Firepower, Priddy's Hard, Gosport, Hampshire PO12 4LE. Tel: 023 9250 5600; www.explosion.org.uk Exhibits range from a late 17th-century matchlock to modern firearms.

The National War Museum of Scotland, The Castle, Edinburgh EH1 2NG. Tel: 0131 225 7534 extension 2201. The Castle houses the regimental museums of the Royal Scots Dragoon Guards and the Royal Scots Regiment, as well as the National War Museum of Scotland.

Wallace Collection, Hertford House, Manchester Square, London W1U 3BN. Tel: 020 7563 9500; www.wallace-collection.com Unrivalled collection of European and Oriental armour and weaponry.

The National Army Museum, Royal Hospital Road, Chelsea, London SW3 4HT. Tel: 020 7730 0717; www.national-army-museum.ac.uk The history of the British Army from 1485 to modern day.

Berwick Barracks, The Parade, Berwick-upon-Tweed, Northumberland TD15 1DF. Tel: 01289 304493 Army barracks dating from 1717–21 containing a permanent exhibition of life in the British Army.

Bosworth Battlefield, Sutton Cheney, Leicestershire CV18 0AD. Tel: 01455 290429 Visitor centre with an interpretation of the battle, replica weapons and battle trail in the country park.